HELICOPTERS

Andrew Langley

An Appleseed Editions book

First published in 2010 by Franklin Watts
338 Euston Road, London NW1 3BH

Franklin Watts Australia
Hachette Children's Books
Level 17/207 Kent St, Sydney, NSW 2000

Created by Appleseed Editions Ltd,
Well House, Friars Hill, Guestling,
East Sussex TN35 4ET

Planning and production by Discovery Books Limited
Designed by D.R. ink
Cover design by Blink Media
Edited by James Nixon

ISBN: 978 1 4451 0028 9

Dewey Classification: 629.1'33352

A CIP catalogue for this book is available from the British Library.

Photograph acknowledgements
Alamy Images: p. 13 bottom (David Gowans); Corbis: pp. 17 top (Tarmizy Harva/Reuters), 17 bottom (John
Van Hasselt); Defence Images © Crown Copyright/MOD, images from www.photos.mod.uk. Reproduced with
permission of the Controller of Her Majesty's Stationery Office: pp. 4 (PO Russell-Stevenson, Royal Navy), 9 bottom
(Cpl Mike Fletcher, Army); European Air Crane: pp. 12, 13 right; Getty Images: pp. 16 (Sandra Teddy), 18 (Luis
Acosta/AFP), 19 bottom (Alan Staats), 22 top (Time Life Pictures), 24 bottom (TG Stock/Tim Graham), 29 top
(David McNew), 29 bottom (Tiziani Fabi/AFP); Istockphoto.com: p. 23 bottom; National Geographic: p. 23 top;
Photolibrary: p. 19 top (Ted Kinsman); Shutterstock: pp. 5 (Maxim Petrichuk), 6, 7 top (Perry Correll), 7 bottom
(Lucian Coman), 8, 10, 11, 14 (David Hancock), 15 top (Robert Kyllo), 15 bottom (Monkey Business Images), 20
(Chris Bence), 21 (Bruno Ismael Da Silva Alves), 22 bottom (Gaetano La Bruzzo), 25 bottom, 26, 27 top; Sikorsky
Aircraft Corporation: p. 9 top (© Sikorsky Aircraft Corporation 2009. All rights reserved); US Navy: p. 27 bottom
(Mass Communication Specialist 3rd Class Paul Perkins); Wikimedia: pp. 25 top (Bernhard Grohl), 28 (USAF).

Cover photos: Shutterstock: top (Sascha Hahn), bottom (Rob Byron).

Printed in China

Franklin Watts is a division of Hachette Children's Books,
www.hachette.co.uk

Contents

What is a helicopter?

A helicopter is an aircraft with no wings. Instead it is lifted up by a spinning set of blades called a **rotor**. The rotor is like a giant **propeller**.

Rotor

A helicopter can fly freely in any direction. It can go straight up or down, and forwards, backwards or sideways. It can even **hover** (stay still) in the air. Very few other aircraft can do that.

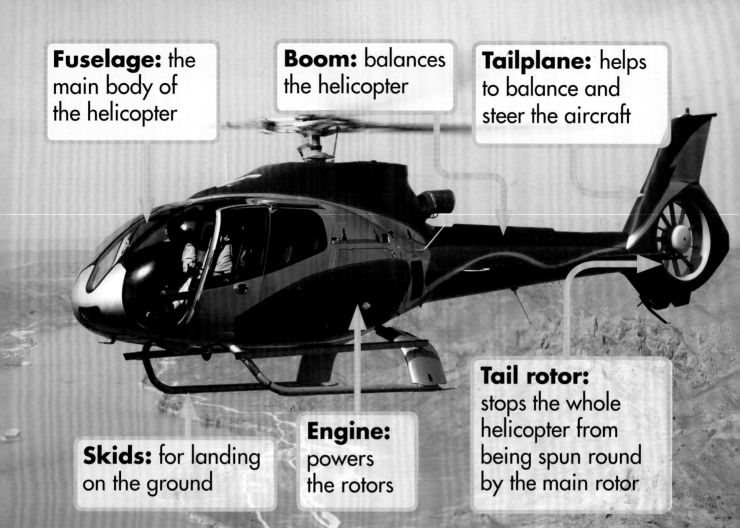

Fuselage: the main body of the helicopter

Boom: balances the helicopter

Tailplane: helps to balance and steer the aircraft

Skids: for landing on the ground

Engine: powers the rotors

Tail rotor: stops the whole helicopter from being spun round by the main rotor

Rotor

The rotor has two or more long blades, set at an angle. As the rotor spins, air travels further over the top of the curved blades than underneath (right). This lifts the helicopter into the air. The pilot alters the angle of the blades to move the helicopter in different directions.

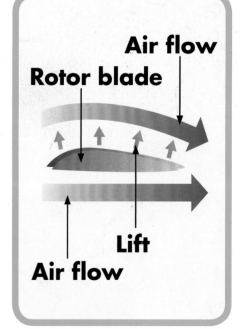

Air flow
Rotor blade
Lift
Air flow

At the controls

The person who controls a helicopter is called the pilot. The pilot sits at the control panel at the front of the helicopter.

There are many types of controls on the panel. Levers and pedals move the helicopter up and down, left and right, or forwards and backwards. Dials and display screens show height, speed, fuel levels and other vital information.

Altimeter: shows height

Rudder pedal

Cyclic control

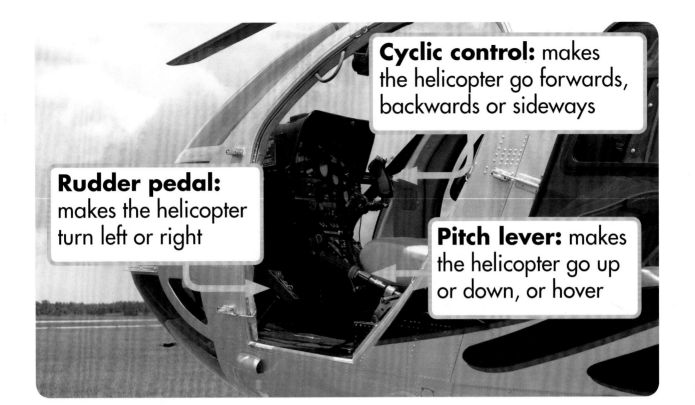

Cyclic control: makes the helicopter go forwards, backwards or sideways

Rudder pedal: makes the helicopter turn left or right

Pitch lever: makes the helicopter go up or down, or hover

Hands and feet

Flying a helicopter is a very skilful job. The pilot has to operate three sets of controls at once – two with his hands and one with his feet.

Large and small

Helicopters can take off and land without a runway. They have more uses than any other aircraft.

There are many different kinds of helicopters in the skies. The smallest can only carry one person (below). The largest helicopters have two rotor blades, and can carry very heavy loads.

World's fastest

The world's fastest helicopter is the Sikorsky X2. It can reach a speed of 288 mph (463 kph) – half as fast as a Boeing 747 jet airliner.

Twin rotors

Helicopters with two rotors do not need a tail rotor to stop the aircraft spinning round. The two rotors rotate in opposite directions. This keeps the helicopter straight.

Passenger helicopters

Helicopters can land in a small space. They are great for carrying passengers over short distances or to places that have no large airfields.

Special landing areas for helicopters are called **helipads**. They are often in unusual places, from office or hotel roofs to offshore oil platforms.

HELIPAD KEEP CLEAR 3

Fuselage

The **fuselage** is the main cabin of the helicopter. All the other parts are attached to it. The pilot and passengers sit in the fuselage.

Into the wild

Mountaintops or remote islands are very hard to reach by plane or land vehicle. But a helicopter can take people almost anywhere.

Flying cranes

Helicopters are ideal for moving awkward and heavy loads. Special helicopters are used as 'flying cranes'.

They lift all kinds of loads, such as long sections of bridge and giant pieces of electricity pylon. Because they hover and fly **vertically**, they can set these items exactly where they are needed.

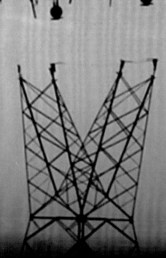

Sling

The load is lifted in a sling or a **cable** attached to the underside of the helicopter. The sling can be raised or lowered.

Aircrane

The S64 Aircrane is one of the strongest of all helicopters. It can lift and carry a load of over 9 tonnes.

Air ambulance

An air ambulance is a helicopter specially equipped to pick up and transport sick or injured people. Helicopters can reach accident scenes faster than ordinary ambulances.

Landing gear

Some helicopters have wheels fixed underneath for landing on. This is called the landing gear. Others are fitted with two long bars, called **skids**.

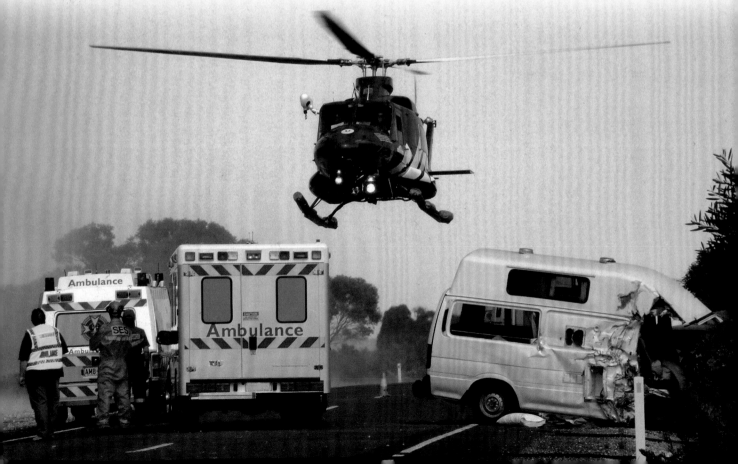

Care in the air

Air ambulances can carry sick people from one hospital to another comfortably and quickly.

They are fitted with medical equipment, so the crew can treat the patient during the flight. Sometimes, a doctor carries out an emergency operation on the spot.

Emergency!

A sailor is trapped on a sinking ship. What's the quickest way to rescue him? Send a helicopter!

Winch

Rescue helicopters have a **winch** fitted to one side. This is a cable which can be lowered to a person on the ground. The person clips onto the cable and is pulled up to the helicopter.

Emergency helicopters can rescue people from all sorts of dangerous situations.

They can also carry vital food and medical supplies to areas hit by disasters, such as earthquakes and floods.

Mountain rescue

In remote mountain areas, teams fly out by helicopter to search for and rescue climbers in trouble.
The teams can even fly at night, using special navigation equipment and powerful lights.

Cops in the sky

Helicopters are very useful to the police. They give a bird's eye view of what is happening on the ground.

The police use helicopters to follow suspected criminals, even those in fast cars. The pilot can tell police cars on the ground where to go.

Heat sensors

At night, police helicopters use **thermal vision** cameras to spot suspects. These show up any object which is giving out heat – such as a human body (right).

Border patrol

Smugglers and immigrants often try to cross borders between countries without being seen. Guards can spot them easily by patrolling border areas in helicopters.

Fighting fires

Wild fires are a big danger in many parts of the world. Firefighters often use helicopters in their battle to put them out.

Helicopters patrol forests to watch for signs of fire.
They drop or spray water on the flames.
They also carry firefighters
to areas on the ground.

Helibucket

Helibucket

A helibucket is a strong cloth bucket on a cable held beneath a helicopter. The pilot hovers and fills the bucket with water from a lake or the sea. Then the water is dumped on to the fire.

Flame guns

Flame guns on helicopters are used to burn strips of forest ahead of the flames. This makes gaps that stop the fire from spreading.

Watching the world

A pilot in the air can see many things we cannot see from the ground. That is why helicopters are used for watching from above.

Radio and TV crews cover news events from the air. On busy roads, pilots see how the traffic is flowing and report jams.

Engineers in helicopters check railway lines, pipelines or power cables for damage (above).

On-board computers

Today's helicopters have computers on board. They work out information, such as the helicopter's position in the air and its speed. This helps the pilot to stay on course and to fly the craft safely.

Aerial shots

Film and TV programme makers use helicopters for shooting scenes. This camera is filming on board a remote-controlled helicopter.

Troop carriers

Helicopters have many roles to play in wartime. This is because they can reach places where ordinary aircraft cannot land.

Big, two-rotor helicopters carry troops, equipment and ammunition. They can even transport **armoured** vehicles. Awkward loads are carried in slings beneath the fuselage.

Biggest ever

The Russian Mil V-12 was the biggest and heaviest helicopter ever built. It was 37 metres long and 12.5 m high – as tall as a house. With a full load, it weighed 97 tonnes.

The hatch

Most transport helicopters have a **hatch** at the rear of the fuselage for loading and unloading cargo. The troops below are about to make a parachute jump from the hatch.

Helicopter gunships

Attack helicopters have a lot of weapons and are called 'gunships'. They have specially armoured bodies.

Helicopter gunships strike at ground targets such as troops, tanks and buildings. The **gunner** sits in a compartment beneath the pilot.

Weapons

Gunships are fitted with rapid-fire cannons, as well as bombs and rockets. They can also fire **air-to-air missiles** against enemy aircraft.

Sub attack

Navy helicopters have special equipment for finding and tracking enemy submarines under the water. They attack them with **depth charges and torpedoes.**

Future helicopters

What will helicopters look like in the future? Engineers are working on new designs which will make them even more useful.

Designers are building **compound planes**. These can take off and hover like a helicopter, but fly forward with propellers or jet engines like an ordinary aircraft. The V-22 Osprey (below) tilts its horizontal rotors vertically like a propeller for forward flight.

Helicopters are being developed (above), which can fly without a pilot. They are controlled by people on the ground.

Backpack helicopters

In the future, we may be able to fly with our own helicopters strapped to our backs. These backpack helicopters have two rotors, spinning opposite ways.

Glossary

air-to-air missile a missile fired from a helicopter at another aircraft

airliner a large plane which carries passengers

altimeter an instrument that shows how high a plane is flying

armoured covered with a layer of tough metal for protection

boom the structure fixed to the rear of a helicopter's main body which carries the rear rotors

cable a strong rope of steel or fibre (a power cable is one which carries electricity)

compound plane an aircraft which is a mixture of a helicopter and an ordinary plane

cyclic control joystick that changes the angle of the helicopter's rotor blades as they spin. It is used to move the helicopter forwards, backwards or sideways

depth charge weapon that explodes when it is dropped under water

fuselage the body of a plane, where passengers or cargo are carried

gunner member of a helicopter crew who operates the guns

hatch an opening with a door in the fuselage of a helicopter for loading goods and people

helipad a special area for helicopters to land on

hover to keep a position in the air without moving in any direction

navigation the following of a planned course to a destination

propeller a set of blades spinning vertically which drive a plane forwards

rotor a set of blades spinning horizontally which lift a helicopter in the air and drive it forwards

rudder pedal the bar moved by the pilot's foot which changes the helicopter's direction

skids the long bars attached underneath a helicopter for landing on

thermal vision seeing an object by sensing the heat it gives out

vertically straight up or down

winch a machine for winding a cable up or down

Index

Websites

**www.williammaloney.com?Aviation/
AmericanHelicopterMuseum/index.htm**
For photos of all sorts of helicopters.

http://science.howstuffworks.com/helicopter2.htm
Watch these videos of a helicopter in flight.

www.exploratorium.edu/science_explorer/roto-copter.html
Make a paper helicopter and test it.